CROSSROADS OF DREAM

PROSE POEMS

Other poetry collections by Anson Gonzalez

*Score*, 1972
*Lovesong of Boysie B. and other poems*, 1974
*Collected Poems 1964-1979*, 1979
*Postcards & Haiku*, 1984
*Moksha: Poems of Light and Sound*, 1988
*Merry-go-round and other poems*, 1992

CROSSROADS OF DREAM

PROSE POEMS

ANSON GONZALEZ

PEEPAL TREE

First published in Great Britain in 2003
Peepal Tree Press Ltd
17 King's Avenue
Leeds LS6 1QS
UK

ISBN 1 900715 89 9

## DEDICATION

To my wife, Sylvia, and my two daughters, Maria and Miguela and in memory of my late son, Miguel (1970) and his one-month sojourn on these planes.

And for Jennifer with special thanks.

Also with thanks and respect to a whole host of others who contributed in ways big and small, but all notable, in helping me shape my art and life, and helping me as far as possible to express aspects of the divine Light and Sound. For a list of these persons, please peruse my *Wall of Gratitude*, which constitutes in a way a litany of the populace who helped me. If I have omitted anyone please forgive the ageing brain.

# WALL OF GRATITUDE

Tony Abraham (d) James C. Aboud Funso Aiyejina Yuklan Akai Hubert Alexander Judy Alcantara Ian Ali M. P. Alladin (d) Eunice Alleyne Garth Alleyne Anthony Allum Bertie Alves Ronald Amoroso Eric Anatol Michael Anthony Charles Applewhaite (d) Hannah Assam Douglas Archibald (d) AVM Owen Baptiste Eddison Baptiste Rhona Baptiste Baptiste-Stephens Family Barataria Boys RC School Lionel Bartolo (d) Lynette Bartolo Betty Basanta J. V. Bastien (d) Keith Belfast Valerie Belgrave Erna Belle Lynette Belle-Smythe Edward Baugh Lennox Bernard Louis Bertrand Sidney Best (b) Selwyn Bhajan Cynthia Birch Judith Blackman Nicole Bland Geraldine Bobb (d) Yvonne Bobb Deanna Boland Isaiah Boodhoo Hyacinth Bonaire Amelda Bourne (d) Kenneth Bourne (d) Brada Brathwaite Kamau Brathwaite Aggrey Brown Dianne Brown Lennox Brown (d) Stewart Brown Br. Book Knolly Butler Eastlyn Bynoe Cheryl Byron (d) Louisa Calio Helen Camps Caratal R.C. School Jan Carew Carnegie Free Library Eddison Carr Lawrence Carrington Wilfred Cartey (d) Terry Cassim Emmanuel Cato (d) Central Library (NALIS) Terry Chandler Monty Chapman Zita Charles Willi Chen Lawrence Chinnia Sylvia Chinnia (d) Ali Chirinos A.M. Clarke (d) Debra Clarke Frank Clarke Moislie Clement CLICO Gilles L. Cobham (d) Trevor Cockburn Glenford Codrington Cuthbert Coerbell Liz Cromwell (d) Gertrude Conception Cloyd Crosby Daphnie Cuffie Marguerite Curtin Astra Da Costa Alvin Daniell Gerald Davis Ralph De Boissiere Claudia de Four Katherine De Frietas Louis De Gale Shirley De Gannes Clara Rosa De Lima (d) Merle des Etages St. Clair Dorant Alex De Verteuil Paul Keens-Douglas Rodlyn Douglas-Lewis Helen Drayton Patrick Dyer Hamlyn Dukhan (d) Sonja Dumas J.D. Elder Erin RC School EXPRESS Newspapers Howard Fergus Calistro Figuero Figuero Family Cheryl Findlay Wilma Forteau First National Bank Gabriel Francis Geraldine Francis (d)

Pat Francis   Hazel Franco   Gloria Francois   Alfred Fraser
Celia Fullerton   Jan Fullerton   Polly Gajadhar   Ancil Gellineau
John George     Wesley Gibbings     Rawle Gibbons     Neville
Giuseppi (d)   Undine Giuseppi   Herman Gill   Ceronne Glasgow
John Otto Goddard   Lorna Goodison   Irma Goldstraw   Albert
Gomes (d)   Evelyn Gonzalez   Otto Z. Gonzalez (d)   Gonzalez
Siblings   Vishnu R. Gosine   Gran Couva R.C. School   Lorraine
Granderson     Granville R.C. School   Linda Greene   Pearl D.
Griffith   Reginald Griffith   Frederick Guerin (d)   Guardian Life
Billie Gustave   Claudia Harvey   George Harvey   Melvina
Hazard   Pat Henderson Allyson Hennessy   Bert Henry   Jeff
Henry   Ronald Henry   Cecil Herbert (d)   Vanessa Herbert Lolita
Hernandez     Joan M. Hewitt     Carlene Hall     Heinemann
Publishers   Errol Hill (d)   Sidney Hill (d)   Merle Hodge   Corinne
Holder   Wilbert Holder (d)   Slade Hopkinson (d)   Ermine
Huggins     Brenda Hughes   Lynette Hutchinson (d) Kendel
Hyppolite   Laurel Ince   Patricia Ismond   David Jackman   Trevor
Jackman   Carl Jacobs   Carol Jacobs   Ramdath Jagessar   Ken
Jaikaransingh   Jamaica Information Services   C.L.R. James (d)
Brian L. James   Cynthia James   Horace James   Renwick James
Albert Jameson (d)     Keith Jardim     Beryl Jeffery (d)   Clarrie
Jeffery (d)   Lucy Jennings   Jean Jeremiah (d)   Debra John   Ronald
John   Joyce John   Amryl Johnson (d)   Astor Johnson (d)   Dorothy
Jolly   Errol Jones   Marilyn Jones   Registe Jordan   Theresa Jordan
Ewart Joseph (d)   Harry Joseph (d)   June Joseph   Ernest Julien
Althea Kaminjolo (d) Romeo Kaseram   Tony Kellman   Jennifer
Amaleta Kernahan   Gladstone King   Jane King   Rupert King
Enid Kirton   Freddie Kissoon   Hollis Knight   Maria Kublalsingh
Makemba Kunle   Roi Kwabena   Treasure La Chapelle   Claudette
La Fortune(d)   Knolly S. La Fortune (d)   Christopher Laird   John
La Rose   Oswyn La Rose (d) Patricia Lashley   Katherine Lawrence
John Robert Lee Lee Pack Siblings   Rosetta Lee Pack (d)   James
Lee Wah   Albert le Veau   Andrea Lewis   Cedric Lindo (d)
Longman Caribbean   Sandra Loregnard   Earl Lovelace   Syl
Lowhar (d) Dave Lum Lock   Indrani Lutchman   Abdul Malik

Karega Mandela   James Manswell   Edward N. Marcelle Kelvin
Marcial (d)   Stanley Marshall   Sybil Maundy (d)   Mausica
Teachers College   Marina Ama Omowale Maxwell   Winston
Maynard Mayo R.C. School Leolyn Millet Therese Mills Eileen
Mc Sween (d)  Ian Mc Donald  Constance Mc Tair  Dionyse Mc
Tair   Roger Mc Tair   Carole Medford   Fitzroy Medina   A.H.
Mendes (d)   Metropolitan Book Suppliers   Ministry of Education
Barbara Mitchell   Aniecia Mohammed Anselma Mohammed
Melinda Mollineaux   Stan Mora     Pamela Mordecai   Paula
Morgan   Mervyn Morris Pamella Mottley-Lawrence   Henry
Muttoo  Ronald Nanton  National Commercial Bank  National
Cultural Council   NBS 610 Radio   Neal and Massy   Brian Ng
Fatt  Lloyd Noel   Thelma Nurse   Old Oak  Monica Ollivierre
Rawlins   Deryck Omar   Karen Omar   Carlton Ottley (d)   Sybil
Ottley   Paula Obe   Donovan Palmer   Palo Seco Government
School   Hezekiah Panchoo   Clive Pantin   Raoul Pantin   Linda
Paponette  Kenneth Vidia Parmasad  Aldwyn Parris  Hamilton
Parris (d)   Steve Parris   Tony Parris   David Perreira   Cherril
Pereira   Sasenarine Persaud   Joyce Peters-Mc Kenzie   Petit
Valley Boys R.C. School   John Pierre  Lizney Pierre   Olman
Pierre   Pamella Pierre Errol Pilgrim  Lorna Pilgrim  Kathleen
Pinder   Yvonne Pinder   Hamida Piralli   Sharon Pitt   Gloria
Pollard  Sandra Pouchet Paquet  Jeremy Poynting  Helen Prada
Presentation College San Fernando   Lloyd Pujadas   Marian
Questel   Victor D. Questel (d)   Radio Trinidad  Jennifer Rahim
Paula Ramberan   Kenneth Ramchand   Peter Ramdhanie (d)
Sidney Ramdial (d)   Evans B. Ramesar   Rajandaye Ramkissoon-
Chen   Balchan Rampaul   Nicole Rampersad   Kenneth
Ramsamooj S.K. Ramsingh (d)  Rosetta Ransome  RBTT Bank
Hazel Redman   Claude Reid (d)   Republic Bank Limited   Br.
Resistance  Elma Reyes (d)   Dawn M. Riley  Maria Rivas  Eric
Roach (d)   Joan Roberts   Philip G. Rochford   Ernest Che
Rodriguez   de Wilton Rogers (d)   Juditha Rogers   Betty
Rohlehr  Gordon Rohlehr  Valerie Romano   Ferdinand Romilly
Angela Roopchand   Glenn Roopchand   Carl Rostant (d)

Arlette Salandy     Andrew Salkey (d)    Krishna A. Samaroo
George K. Sammy  Kim Sammy  Roderick Sanatan  Reinhard
Sander  Wilmot Sanowar  Calvin Saunders  Clifford Sealy (d)
Alfred Sealey (d)   Samuel Selvon (d)   Leslie Sawh  Ruth Sawh
Olive Senior   A.J. Seymour (d)    Joanna Shaw-Lloyd    Errol
Sitahal  Fitzroy Shepherd  Stephanie Shurland (d)  Eintou Pearl
Springer  Janet Stanley Marcano  Gemma Stapleton   Lionel St
Aubyn (d)  Verlia Stephens  John Stewart  Van S. Stewart  St.
George's College  Caps St. Hill (d)  Stork St. Hill (d)  Hayden
Strasser  Judy Stone   Jean Sue Wing  Genevieve Superville
Conrad Syriac    TASK    Rudolph Taylor (d)    Harold M.
Telemaque (d)  Ramdath Thackorie (d)  Cheziah B Thompson
Neila Todd   Tortuga R.C. School   Alana Trafford  Trinidad
Public Library   UWI School of Continuing Studies   Valsayn
Teachers College    Alfred Wafe   Anthony Walcott   Derek
Walcott  Barbara Walker  Rosanne Walker  Anne Walmsley
Cassandra Ward  Ingrid D. Washington  Margaret Watts  Roy
Watts (d)  Victor Watty (d)  Winston Welch  Lisa Wells  Efebo
Wilkinson  George Williams  Howard Williams (d)  Marie Ella
Williams    Rudy Williams   Rose Willock   Ronnie Wilson
WITCO  Auburn Wiltshire  Louis Woodruffe  Carol Worme
Ermine Wright (d)    Writers Union of Trinidad and Tobago
(WUTT)

# CONTENTS

Gerontion and his mate take more than twenty-four hours to do a day of nothing. It's so exhausting to achieve this from forced and habitual rising around six, to listening to the morning local talk show while browsing for email, which could be disheartening when his friends contemplate their navels too much and forget to remember him. Then a small breakfast, which his wife feels she must get up to make for him – hopsbread sandwich and tea without milk or sugar, which he has enlivened by buying several varieties of tea for different mornings. Arguing about the news follows, with him never being able to abide her views, then his going to buy newspapers, sometimes 3 or 4 which he can ill afford and which take him well into the afternoon to read. This is interrupted, of course, by checking for email, ICQ, or Peoplelink, or answering mail, or promising to write in his dream journal after having long forgotten the dream and being unable to decipher it to see whether it was a healing, a prophetic dream, guidance, a karmic resolution, an initiation, or a spiritual adventure. Things like making a doctor's or dentist's appointment are put on the back burner, always until tomorrow. There is the habitual trek to the post office, or drive rather, to check the box for junk mail, utility and credit card bills and pension cheques at month end. Sometimes to relieve his wife's persistent and continuous work and lamentation, he washes the dishes, vacuums some rooms, cuts the lawn or clears the grating at the corner after the neighbourhood's rubbish piles up, especially after rain. On evenings, he usually tries to chat and lime with the wife between 4 and 8 pm., after which they retire to their own tvs. He usually watches something mindless, basic and action filled; she turns to something equally vacuous of her taste. Before they know it, the spirit of night attacks their eyelids and tired bodies and they can barely turn off the ever-present remote controls to drift on a sea of darkness, sampling the forever sleep till the dawn remarkably tickles their eyelids, so they can start the cycle again.

Did you hear the drums this morning? Their rhythm rises to a staccato crescendo, waking the valley, telling of the return of spirits to ethereal realms, deserting bodies captured nightlong, now flying in the lightening darkness, and allowing mundane spirits to again inhabit their corporeal abodes.

His heart echoes their rhythm, under control; think of the two hearts beating in you, possessed as it were, by another spirit, as, in a sense, three unseen dancers frolic in the dark. Those drumbeats could well be the hearts of your house, like drums sounding in his head, summoning him to worship at your feet.

You are his earth goddess, his sister, his sweetheart, his wife, his unattainable representative woman, the missing link in his soul. Thoughts of you are the cymbal, which summon him to your side, in spirit or in flesh, which make him find and lose his reason for living.

Would you were a spirit goddess, so that summoning drums could make you possess his body this moment, displace his soul, as you fuse your bodies, though on awakening he may only retain dreamlike memories of the powers you give; like an exhausted devotee in the lightening dark, the morning would find him fulfilled.

The drums are dying in desultory diminuendo. Do the barking dogs bid farewell to devotee or spirit? Isn't it always that the faithful follower and the worshipped deity must finally separate on the tenuous fibres of hope?

The morning comes, and hopefully it is the glorious day of fulfilment. The poet-lover looks to the east for the rising face of his love in the sun. The drums are packed away, the spirits have fled, and the hushed cadence of dawn is pregnant with love and hope.

Babble from communication towers stultifies the ear, nullifies logic and embalms the sensitivity to any further concern for communal life. Putrid hate pervades the Babel towers that lift in blue space, reaching beyond the skies but forgetting to reach for God and Love... God (Itself/Himself/Herself) is rendered so helpless that screaming fanatics seize his cause from his helpless hands and smash to smithereens churches, synagogues, masjids, temples. On his behalf they consign infidels to perdition, gaining for themselves putative harems... and every nanosecond the babble continues, bells ring, ring, ring...

Best dressed, dominant, skilful steps, graceful movements, desired, admired and envied by all. Variations on a heel and toe, one-two one-two-three, twist, turn, flaunt, with much coquetry in gestures and facial expressions.

Satisfied with her virtuosity, her flamboyance, satisfied with the obeisance of her courtiers and ladies, confident that she has out-danced them all, outlasted them all, she approaches the drummers. With a dramatic flourish, she stops the drums. She acknowledges the acclaim. Plaudits fill the air. This *la reine*, this queen! Until the next soirée or belaire dance.

Tomorrow she has to clean and wash for her masters.

In a little town dedicated to books, we spent a few hours on a Sunday browsing picturesque avenues of bookshops with specialist and non-specialist ones. The first shop visited (because it was near where we parked) was a poetry bookshop, which contained as many poetry books as any good-sized library. I bought two items, but could have bought many more. As we traversed the town, a thunder of colourful motorcyclists vibrated the main streets like so many bumble bees looking for honey; not the Hell's Angels types, more benign but still intimidating; they caused the post-service natives and the window-shopping bibliophiles to stand on the pavements and wonder. When their parade diminished, we proceeded like book pilgrims (well at least I did) to the various shops, searching for whatever called. In this cornucopia of papier the feasts bedevilled the eyes and challenged the pockets. I could only get one more item as the pound is the most expensive currency in the world... Treasuring my collection I left the peculiar town which is, otherwise, just a little Welsh town, to ride the beautiful Welsh landscape back to the capital, Cardiff – and a three-hour nap. The books, all poetry criticism and history, especially on prose poetry, will satisfy me for some time.

I have become obsessed with cleaning out my bedroom and library of clutter and things that have no practical purpose. I need to convert my library to a study so that I can get out of the bedroom into an ambience that promotes reading, study, writing and scholarship. Here in the bedroom there are too many books and papers. The papers, maybe precious, that I've published and printed (or rejected) are deteriorating with age – poems, stories, articles. They have become dried out and crumbly; little beings are living in them, having their fill and spreading to other books and papers. Several large garbage bags of past-life episodes have been shredded and sent onward – perhaps to new life as papier mache – who knows? – or to be burnt on the dunghills of oblivion. I had saved all my cheques for decades, and the cheque books too... lying there, taking up precious space, a negative tribute to an artist's ineptness, to an indifferent financial record and life. Still, I could harvest from them all the cheques given out as prizes or scholarships to aspiring writers, and even to accomplished ones. These are culled from the more mundane payments to IRS, utilities, doctors, chemists, labs, schools and supermarkets that make up the bulk of my involvements these long years past. Sometimes I salvage things which mark certain episodes in my life, certain passages that pleased or pained, stumbling blocks or stepping stones. Soon everything will be thinned out. It will be light and airy... and I will have no excuse to put off the few moments of lucidity and creativity afforded me.

He didn't think their careers should be jeopardized because they didn't master English. They never speak it anyhow. Some departments, like the kitchen, hardly use it. But they develop "sweet hand" and get rave reviews in culinary magazines. And they pamper your palates, even if they can't use the proper past tense or participles. You understand them well as you seek a second helping.

He is the feeble father of his daughters' eyes, about whom they are very concerned. Whether he is well enough, bored, in need of anything? They are so solicitous of his well being – but a bit overzealous about controlling his diet. And his beer sampling. Nevertheless, they give him a good feeling, and a wholesomeness that usually evades him. At the same time they are not mushy, emotional creatures. They have strong feelings and emotions, sentiments and philosophies on life. They know what they want and have planned how to achieve it. It is refreshing to associate with these young women, his daughters, who have given him the name of father. One evening they went for a bonding walk on the bay. It ended a quiet, pleasant day filled with filial affection. It was the signature of his visit to them.

December came with its many distractions, as people engrossed themselves in activities designed to entrench desire for the attachments of the world, to the detriment of soul, all in the name of a reborn god of two millennia.

Practically compulsory socializing and celebrating filled the ethers with negative vibrations of a forced jollity. All around, it passed as expressions of tradition. To resist it increased the pressure of the astral force, as the aloneness of one's spirit, dulled to Spirit, alienated oneself from man, souls, Soul and therefore God. To flow with it dulled the spirit in enervating exercises that fed on gluttony, inebriation, waste, greed and physical-level fellowship.

Mouthed words of goodwill, that evaporate before the Epiphany, stir only dimly a message and a meaning of Love that soul tries wanly to reactivate and pass to Mind, so that the organism may gain balance along the course of its journey.

Spiritual exercises – alone in this maelstrom of a long continuing season of lust and other perversions that rise to a crescendo in February – are the soul's balm. They put Soul in touch with the Spirit. It touches that base, which is the foundation of all life, which emanates from Godhead, Ocean of Love and Mercy. It shines its myriad, but universal Light, spreading its energy, that Logos, the Shaba Dhun, that together expresses ultimate Love, in the very reason for our existence, the love of the Lord that wills it.

So the outer seasons of time come and pass, but the inner, eternal season of Love exists in the absoluteness of the relationship between Soul, Guru and God.

He watches himself degenerate. Slowly his hair floats away in the wind like silk cotton seeds. His face tanned by wind, weather and worry becomes a shield against life's inconsistencies. His muscle tone softens like Mr. Biswas's calves, flapping as he moves. He strains against the slightest objects his wife asks him to move. His back creaks like a rusty door hinge in a mysterious old house in a horror story when he tries to lift a bag of cement that he used to hike nonchalantly onto his shoulders. He smiles knowingly as Dr. Sawh, the urologist, talks about old men's denial of loss of girth and power because of that activated gland brought on by the years. And by karma he adds. He grudgingly visits Dr. Tim, for dental rehabilitation, to present a pleasant smile at a child's graduation. He grimaces as he eats the tasteless, spiceless food that is now his dietary regimen to control the clogging veins that Dr. Ronald temporarily unclogged, like WASA's units which malfunction with their usual effect on the body civic. He meets a young woman, rosy cheeked and vital. She smiles with openness. The triggers go off in his head or somewhere. There is no effect. He has forgotten what he used to do.

This season, as usual, our forgotten language has been dusted out, and received a period of exposure before it hibernates once more. The annual Parang festival brings out groups old and new, some old compositions and some new ones in more standard Spanish; so paeans of La Virgen Maria, La Anunciación, and La Navidad reverberate around the countryside until January 6. They have been strongly challenged by the still new phenomenon called soca parang/ parang soca which retains the rhythms and some of the melodies but have no religious significance and are sometimes just simple double entendre, like: *Ah want mih brekfas in mih bed/ gimme black pudding instead.*

They are a whole new genre and liven up the parties of sensualists who couldn't care less whether Xmas falls on Ash Wednesday because it's just an interlude before carnival when the real bacchanal begins. Sometimes he wishes he wasn't so dissociated and that he could drink his arse full of rum and fete the whole four months away without thinking about responsibility, bills, family, other people, debt and disease. But he knows that if he tries, in midst of it all, a little voice will keep asking him: is this your purpose for living?

All the punnanies are destined to pass him by, because he has already answered the call...

Love for persons, like love for life, is sometimes realized or activated by the strangest incidents. Many times it arises out of misfortune. Out of the depths of despair soul cries to its creator for salvation, and because of the creator's love for soul, a perennially new bond is strengthened. Soul revels in its newly found unity with its source and glows in the warmth of spirit.

At the physical plane something similar happens: A crisis brings people together and the soul-sparks in the eyes sometimes touch. The call for help, and the desire to assist, come together and generate love, simulating the events on the soul plane. When this is based on pre-existing mutuality, emotions erupt and this-plane love is born with all its adjuncts of desire, pleasure and possession and all of its attendant pains when the situation is not really open to such love.

Expression of love on this plane should not be blocked; channelled, yes, but not blocked. To stem the flow, to dam up the love within one's heart, is to make it turn rancid and sour.

Once love starts flowing, with its healing aspects, its stroking aspects, one must enjoy it in the fullness of spirit. One must view it as an aspect of divinity that takes it course towards the goals of self-realization and God Realization. One must love and learn. One must live and learn. And what one must learn from all this is how to love.

Golden thoughts, golden acts, golden memories, golden associations. Black is beautiful, golden. My daughters are beautiful, gilded.

Soul is beautiful, God-loved. Some friends are golden; gilded. Their smiles can change the aura of the world. Most babies are golden. Except they grow up, and lately, as they become killers, are argent, till they understand. To be golden, to be gilded, is their heritage. People promise their spouses golden companionship. They live long and tarnish sets in. They are no longer golden, nor gilded; argent, bronze, maybe. They should have died young, and golden. But in their deepest recesses, memory of gold lingers. The guru comes and reminds them of their golden heritage.

Small islands may not always be able to compete with grand continents and metropolises. Somehow our islands have managed to produce Nobel laureates, acclaimed authors, actors, world-class athletic champions, world boxing champions, beauty queens, artists, musicians, scholars and leaders. Pride of this particular island nation, however, is the invention of the steel band or steel drum band, as those in the north are wont to call it. Here the instruments are called "pans" or "steel pans".

The romantic history of its invention by the marginalised urban folk, who seized dustbins and oil barrels to make music for the carnival (because the skin drums and the bamboo stalks – tambour bamboo – were outlawed) is epic.

Through the decades since the 1930s, these humble drums were developed into instruments that paralleled those of the traditional orchestra, and the bands are now often referred to as orchestras and ensembles.

This development and the skill necessary to play these instruments have universally impressed everyone. At least one American has achieved the standard of virtuosity, but the acclaimed players and bands are from the islands. Indeed Islandman's home is known worldwide as the Mecca of the Steelband.

Others had gone off to the grazing grounds. El Viejo, the old one, stayed in the shade ruminating, being unproductive. He's lost his force, too weak now to frighten off the young bulls. His mind wavers as he thinks of wandering off into the wilderness to eke out his days. Now there's no harem to protect , defend and dominate; no calves to beget. Now, he's threatened by predators grown fearless; only the waiting for the unknown end remains.

Months fly like migratory swallows flitting their winter sojourns for short weeks over the warm clime, waiting for the changing pole of the world to right itself in the vernal equinox.

So soul, trapped in a body in the autumn of its days, sees the time of its passage draw near, and wonders whether more migrations will recur or whether the final migration is at hand.

Body, ascendant, plays tricks to trap soul for one more round (at least). It seeks advantage in excuses: its ageing and therefore increased tiredness, which inhibits soul's practise of exercises that lead to its liberation from these coils; social obligations, which break soul's contemplation of the spiritual worlds, and engrosses it in lower-world shackles; physical needs, which cut into the time and energy available for obtaining its spiritual needs; professional requisites, which call for a consumption of time, energy and thought to satisfy lower-world commitments.

All of these soul tries to convert into spiritual acts of commitment to guru and God, so that each event and activity, each thought, each effort to remain focused on the path, each failure in adhering to the Path, would lead soul towards its real goals of soul realization and God realization. Soul tries to achieve a balance in favour of its evolution, so that, transcendent, it will become the prime mover of all activity in this world.

Little acts cumulate – resulting in often unobserved miracles of guidance, healing and blessing. Soul begins to win some rounds on the inner, and this is manifested on the outer.

The coconut tree near the road had been cut down and the poui opposite was blooming. The poui was the pride of the village. It was planted there by a governor's wife a long time ago. The village idlers loitered beneath it and played draughts – sometimes wappie and rummy.

There are three main buildings at Bonne Aventure Junction: Sooklal's shop and parlour and Deen's shop and bar on the western side, and Popo's shop on the eastern side. The other buildings are hidden by bush and high hibiscus fences.

We lived in Popo's shop for about five years. Popo and Deen were brothers and bitter rivals in business and agriculture. Deen was more successful, so Popo moved away to try business elsewhere and we rented his place. We started to run a dry goods shop too. From a stool in Deen's bar I looked through the window at Popo's place where I used to live. The "Vote Jack Kelshall" sign from an election many years ago was faded but still up. The building was as ramshackle as ever but I remembered the good times I spent there. I looked at the standpipe in front of Popo's place and I could almost see Milly fetching water at night and I sneaking through a hole in our fence to whisper or kiss, if it was safe.

There was also Agatha who lived next door. I remember the trouble we caused between our families. I could also remember the day the police came to arrest her uncle, Roy. He was a big sagaboy in the village but the police seized all his clothes. He had got them from the white people's clotheslines at Pointe-a-Pierre where he used to work as a handyman.

Under Popo's shop the barber with his box of tools on his bike was still working, while Popo spoke to him in Hindi.

Just then a taxi came up and I shook hands and left Deen and Ganga. Popo still looked across at them with envy.

Labara in his dream world flapped in cosmic wind like welcoming bunting, but no one who was invited entered. He peered through portals but the driveway was always empty. He thought he heard a knock and sat up in anticipation. It was only uninvited visitors.

Your absence weighed heavily on his dream mind. Dawn and reality rushed at him implacably. He awoke to a frustrating Antillean routine; darkened by the absence of your gaze.

Ladies and gentlemen ... as they come to the centre of the ring... Boysie is fighting Himself desperately; Himself looks anaemic. He hasn't been training. He hasn't been treating himself right. Himself can hardly win this fight. Boysie and Himself are now standing in the centre of the ring. They are trading lefts and rights with tremendous power. Neither is giving ground ... Ladies and gentlemen, did you hear that noise? Something terrible has just happened. The ring has fallen about the heads of the antagonists. The audience has streamed out of the hall. Only a lone lady stands over Himself saying, "You almost made it", over and over again. Ladies and gentlemen, as the custodians come forward, I bid you ... Goodnight...

When spring is there, yellow poui flowers and crimson immortelles emboss hillsides and roadsides here, where miraculously some flourish till summer. Summer. Time of the flambouyants, which bloom till October, from Trinidad in the south to the Caymans at the end of the arc.

First there was the follower. He was numbed in the cathedrals of hope. Statuary bored him. Then they scared him. The gay priests upset him. Not because they were gay, but because they preached against it. Tobacco-stained teeth and yellow-stained fingers as they turned the missals turned him off. Drunken ones were pissed. Unchaste ones were unclean. Especially the one whose son died recently. And he didn't mean the one on the cross. One day, a bloody, tortured bust, thorn-crowned, suddenly grinned at him. He left the church and began his search for a different path. Since then he has been a seeker.

B.   So a song lights up a heart. So a poem tells a truth.
     So one person touches another's soul and leaves a mark
     indelible.

She. (is silent)

B.   So I seek a truth elusive. So I seek a love conclusive
     So one person touches another's soul and leaves a mark
     indelible.

She. (is silent)

B.   Fear not the touch of sweet affection. Fear not the tensely
     held attraction.
     So one person touches another's soul and leaves a mark
     indelible.

She. (is silent)

B.   (shakes his head and slowly...)

He lost his mother's love while her milk still flowed.

Another provided succour and caring. He learned to accept love wherever he found it. His displaced heart absorbed love like a sponge until it started to leak. His heart's love valve could not be repaired by any amount of caring. In attempts to staunch the flow he became an overachiever. His finger in the dyke was his achievements at school, in sports, in academia and his professions. The more he achieved, the faster love leaked. No amount of adulation could stem the tide that threatened to breach his being.

He gained the love of a devoted woman. Her showering of love flowed through the cracks but his love-leak threatened his well-being.

Doctors of church, family and friends could not staunch the leak, so he kept pumping more love into his arid heart till it exploded in his face when the cigar was pulled from the hole.

Dear Bill, with his stepchild smile and endearing visage, could always find love wherever he found himself. In his many circles love assailed him, though he tried to escape her blandishments.

Poor Bill. Will he ever get his heart's cure now he's run out of ambition and things to accomplish? I bleed for my soul brother. We both suffer from the stepchild syndrome – the forever leaking heart.

Laden with karmic burdens, weighted with debts unpaid, ledgers to be balanced, additional debts incurred, the expected glow of bliss is tarnished in the process of learning to love all life. To be – a painful process. When the gaze of human consciousness rests upon the hurting edges of union, it's hurt diminishes. The joint journey through the passage of night is wracked with pain of fear, misunderstanding, betrayal, loss and doubt. There are times when the Light pierces the fog – in the eyes of offspring blossoming. But then the sound filters through, blessing situations, salving wounds, in preparation for another passage of strenuous education towards becoming the individual self. Itself to become the Self – the One.

Same address for four decades – stability or inertia? One job since sixteen – virtue or failure? Never lived or studied abroad – limited or contented? His old car and he – together for twenty-five years. Same wife and children for forty years – long term commitment or fear of change? Can he go into the next plane – or will he be attached forever to this one and haunt it eternally? Same heart beating beating from birth.

He grew up in the countryside. It was always nice and fresh. Lots of greenery and other colours. Smells and textures. Generally wholesome. He only knew about ghettoes when he read *Child of the Jago* – it was so unreal. Poverty around him was usually bearable. People had a quiet dignity and a sense of respectability, and their place in the community. If they asked you to go to the shop to buy them some meagre provisions – like a pennyworth of tobacco and a cent of salt – you couldn't refuse. He lived in many places like this during his long life. It was not till late in life, his late twenties, that he first encountered a ghetto. There was this famous warrior-priest-drummer that they had to visit in the Governor's Estate. Despite the reputation of the Estate, and its fear-generating atmosphere, they conducted folk-cultural business and left within the hour. Safe, yes – but with a sudden hacking cough, runny eyes and nose. He wondered at the genetic inheritance of a people who could survive, apparently unscathed, such an environment. As he took to his fevered bed, he thought that if these people could survive the Middle Passage and the plantations, a rundown ghetto would hardly challenge them.

The avant-garde artist attended the Writers Group meeting. He distributed little poem-cards to the poet members. The cards were symbolic scenes. The reverse side of each card was the back view of the front. The poets looked at them. They read the captions. They looked at the verso and the recto. They looked at one another. They looked at the poet-artist and lowered their eyes.

The gentle poet outlasted the century. The millennium was too much for him. Not only the body but also the mind was stressed. The culture overtook him. His aesthetic environment had degenerated. A calypsonian beat him for his rent. He tried to maintain his gentility. Became a symbol of a past age existing only in memory. One day he forgot to wake up.

They have fifty or sixty offspring scattered around the country and through time. Parallel common-law concubinage has valleys and distant villages filled with barely acknowledged offspring. Much unintentional incest must be occurring. Unrecognized siblings exchanging hearts unbeknownst to thoughtless fathers whose seeds spring up like knotgrass and *ti marie* in unknown savannahs. That handsome couple on Charlotte Street, looking like siblings, the woman pregnant, makes me wonder.

Vibrations stir him, make him smile, make him patient. He's like a puppy waiting for its owner to rub its tummy. Rub his head. Fondle his ears. He rolls over in pleasure, short or long. He didn't think that the mistress had been away so long; his ears perk up, his tail wags, he sniffs with delight and leaps at her with joy. Separation is always forgotten on greeting. Silence is always worth it when broken. He licks her feet, hands, neck, cheeks. He's beside himself with joy.

It's no joke; we sat and waited in the dim porch, surrounded by floral friends. Souls shared beauty and love with their gifts. Greeted in gratitude they soften the attitude. Yellow thryallis and pink pentas enliven the pathway with their neighbour hibiscus, the dwarfed and the tall; ixora of the stunted view, flowers of shade and hue shelter under bougainvilla proud. The path is horticultural heaven. On this special evening the lady of the night kept us waiting. On this magic night, Cinderella Cereus set to bloom, to show her innate colours, to shower us with beaming flowers. Like impatient children we were rewarded with special sight – a once-a-year blossoming of spirit at work. By morning they had wilted like jaded lovers; but for one glorious moment they opened us to the wonder of the universe.

Two of his grandmothers were as brown as balatas and just as sweet and hardy. The third was as black as a nutmeg, and hardy and as seasoned as love. So was her black husband. Redman's father was brown but had two red brothers and two red sisters among the horde of siblings. One Xmas, another relative, his father's aunt on the Simon branch, whom they had never heard of before, visited. She had a hideous scar, a macfan, they said, where another relative had split her head open for her small inheritance of cottage and land. She brought a boy and girl with her, black, with strong beautiful white teeth, who caused us all to damage our teeth in response to their challenge to crack xmas almonds in our mouths. Then there was his birth mother, an attractive Latina-looking woman, and his stepmother, whom he always called Mammy. Until he was in his sixties he never realised that she looked Indian. And that, only after his Sino-latina sisters told him, after his mother's funeral, that their mother, our mother, had said that the Indian woman had taken him away from her.

A couple resembling Mannie Ramjohn and his wife came to Joe's house. They said they wanted to visit and stay with Joe and his wife. Joe's wife was affronted because she had never heard of them before. Hard words erupted between Joe and his wife. She refused, adamantly. The couple ran toward the coconut tree in the front yard and disappeared. They fused with the coconut tree. Became frond people. A coconut frond woman reached out and stroked Joe's wife's face. Another coconut frond circled Joe's waist and coconut frond fingers caressed his bald head.

In that period of night turning morning, at the crossroads of dream and conscious awareness, he turned in her arms and kissed her welcoming lips. Sweetness pervaded his being. He was suffused with bliss by her reciprocation. He remembered that he had never tasted her fully sharing lips nor felt her darting tongue (maybe sweeter than he imagined), but this reality was palpable. Her comforting was mixed with eroticism and maternity as her right nipple slipped into his mouth, and he nibbled, thinking of biblical proverbial pomegranates, or, as he prefers, luscious pears. These are much sweeter (as again he thinks that the reality would be just as sweet). Her spilling juices tickled his nostrils outer and inner; and he caressed the mound of her tummy, so exquisite to the touch, and so entrancing. Her hands gently led his head to her fount, and there he stayed and pleasured her, till the morning sunrise peeped through the window and joined in their pleasure as it sensually licked his face and woke him. Her presence slowly faded, leaving a lingering smile on his face...

Later in the morning he was preparing a sermon. He came across a reading that said that when we dream of marriage and mating it represents an inner initiation or a closer tie at a different level with the Holy Spirit.

Is she his matrix with the Divine?

East – region of mystery and beauty. Marco Polo first extolled its wonder and wealth in the west. Magic caught imagination and sparked an age of exploration. Men sought her from all corners of sea and land. Columbus started something different, placing east in west. Today spice of the east resides in central. Magic still fascinates – of skin, eyes, texture, hair, of vibrant personality and mystic allure. Like Polo he hungers and thirsts for spice, but the journey is short. She is in the centre of the country and of his heart.

Faux cane-cutter in red house. White hall. Presidential palace. Palm as soft as lambskin mittens wielding irons. Palms sticky as Brer Rabbit's tar baby. No psoriasis from cane-cutting fibres. Perfumed and bedecked in finest damask. Spitting, snarling, no alley-cat. A Persian pretending tigritude. Imperious. Word reified and deified. *Primus super pares*. Friends count for little. Off with their heads. Kill Damon. Kill Pythias. El Supremo hasta la muerte.

Body parts of poems in dim brain laboratory; stored in refrigerated bins. Metaphors to create the spines of Mr. and Mrs. Frankenstein. Poems bubble and pulse in amber electrical liquids. Innumerable metaphors held here. The poetic researcher is excited. There are brains – the topics that will run the poems before the eyes of (in)discriminating readers. Hearts that imbue the poems with passion to move both poet and audience. Muscles, sinews, bones, skins and hair. Put together. Connected to tubes of poetic texture. Professor Poet tries to get things right. Buttons are pushed, beakers of rhythms bubble and flow. In anticipation, the final switch is thrown. A tremor strikes the Frankenstein poems. They rise. Grotesque beauty. Professor Poet covers his eyes. The poems break out from the poetry laboratory and flee into the wider world. Prof hurries after them with a dose of metonymy in his hands.

I want to sing songs for you, Trinidad and Tobago. I want to find songs that lift the mind and soul. Not songs to make you wine in monotonous, automatic kinetic response as at carnival, that celebration of the tinsel and the tawdry. It is a communion I seek, a soaring – a celebration of being that combines and encapsulates the love of self, citizen, country and deity. Here, where we have more religions and churches, temples, mandirs and masjids than our size permits and our behaviour suggests, the soul is smothered in negativity.

One weekend sixteen finalists competed in the island's national stadium, named after the island's Olympic gold medal sprinter, to select the champion youth steelband of the nation. Five soloists would settle the matter of who was to be crowned best pannist and future virtuoso. Imagine, if you will, sixteen bands/orchestras of at least 50 players (i.e. 800 players) performing for the evening. Imagine their evolved instruments, no longer discarded rubbish bins, but chromed silver and gold, of various sizes, shapes and combinations, skilfully toned and tuned to represent the assorted sounds of a full orchestra. Imagine the unexpected sounds and dulcet tones of ranges and octaves, emanating from among the glister reflected on the instruments by the setting sun. Imagine the cool sea-breeze wafting in, enhancing the atmosphere of electric competition and instrumental virtuosity. Imagine child musicians, from six to eighteen, rendering the compositions of contemporary nationals (Daniel, Sharpe, Samaroo, Teague etc.) and the vintage classics of Europe (Bach, Beethoven, Liszt, Handel etc). Children playing well above their chronological age and expected ability. Everyone a star; everyone together – a constellation; making steelband music a pleasure and a treasure of the nation.

Who won or lost the various categories was immaterial. The legacy of the steelband – in good hands in this millennium.

He doesn't have it in him to be in love. Being in love requires time, energy, future, hope and promise. He could only be dessert, entertainment perhaps, a decoration, like old wine, perhaps to be imbibed on a special occasion or two. To be vaguely remembered; wistfully, as the good old times. After a lifetime of service, duty, fatherhood, provenance, husbandry, all in the name of love, there is merely time and energy enough to salvage the negatives created, and shape them into booty for the next passage. There is no hope, future, promise here. Only a fantasy of what might have been.

Infatuation lags far behind the concern and consideration he has for you. His desire is a serious affection that is prepared to stem all storms; that is reasonable and yet unreasonable. It is offered as a boonful gift that is yours without need to return. It makes him vulnerable to you, as he wants to be anyhow, with the capacity to hurt and be hurt. He wants you to take him, whatever is left. He wants you to treat him specially, tenderly, as a helpless bird, or else with mocking anger you can crush his manhood and leave him forlorn and broken ...

There were masters old and new, renowned, international and local in the Cardiff museum and art gallery. But what impressed him most were some sculptures by Rodin. The power and passion of "The Kiss", in black bronze, larger than life, as emotive as the narrative of the lovers on/in Keats's Grecian Urn, really caught his attention and demanded his contemplation. The power and passion he imagines that always eludes. The response he idealizes, that he can share as the figure did/does, or experience with another, in a moment present-past-future, timeless, engraved in eternity, in the museum of time, that says: Here we have lived, and loved (and paid for it). For a brief moment transfiguration took place as he tried to place his loves in the vale of perdition and he to their rescue regardless of cost and his own destiny...soon interrupted by the marshals indicating that the museum is closing and they must move to the exit. Saved he was from deciding which or whether he would, like Dante, enter hell to save another.

He told the girl next to him in the stands at the Carifesta parade, "This place is so great!" The middle-aged white lady smiled and waved ten feet up in the air on stilts. Moko jumbies they call stilt walkers here, after the African tradition. Like phantoms bearing the vengeance of Moko. Dancing to the kaiso music like a bat out of hell. Rhythm rhythm rhythm. Riddum riddum riddum (as Resistance offspring would say). She balanced on one leg and danced the other like Kitchener making his dingolay. People would say she was to the manor born. Petit bourgeosie. Bottle blonde with a touch of the tar brush (as De Boissiere would say). But fully fitting, her perfect self, with a background of dance and culture, trained and native, and in this case trained in and by the native. On the promenade, in the savannah, on the road, at the stadium (now named after Crawford). Among a band of black children and youth. All delicately and skilfully, but evenly balanced, floating in the air, gyrating, hopping, dancing the carnival, dancing the spirit. The white lady at one with them. Sharing a bottle of water, a congratulatory pat, camaraderie. He stood and applauded. The stand stood and cheered. This place great, yes.

Was it the laureate frolicking in the vast sea, then tossed hither and yon by some behemoth of the deeps? The waters churned from nature and the actions of the beast. The laureate laughed at first, then grew mortally afraid from the attacks of both beast and sea. His cries allayed the waters, where monstrous waves, flecked with foaming froth, were a terrible beauty. The sea changed its furore and subsided. The blue waters turned green, and the foam, still beautiful, lost its menace. The behemoth dived and disappeared. The poet floated in the emerald water, spent and wondering what had happened and what it meant. The observer could not make head or tail of the incident – what did the waters mean, what did the behemoth signify, why the change of colours? Why did the poet remain in the calm green waters?

Before he goes on stage at the poetry reading he freezes. Becomes apprehensive. So much of it is performance. Razzle-dazzle and glaze. People revelling in superficialities. Superficies of things. Looking first for the big jokes. They didn't leave their houses to be subtle. Not here in this crass place. They laugh at tragedies and cruelties, as at age-old jokes and malapropisms. The demotic rules. Could be PhDs, professors, prophets, pundits or pastors. Themselves laughing as they perform their own cons. So standing there, looking bold and confident, in the *Soca Boat*, having to share works suitable to the occasion – among rapso artists, limbo dancers, bongo dancers, steelpan players, raunchy comedians, soca artistes, rock artists, black rock artistes – he chose something that Derek called one of those calypso-kind-of things (unworthy of his poetic potential). Mark Strand and Joseph Brodsky, feeling his discomfort, had softened the blow and said that he should always write for the angels. At the *Soca Boat* the variegated audience stared quizzically at the old red-skinned poet, teetering on the cusp of tolerance and rejection, moving back and forth between tolerance and animosity, their vibrations smacking his face like the tide that lapped, lapped the port outside and receded and returned. So he gave them some razzle-dazzle, populist pieces, deploying the demotic, focusing on the folk, swizzling a callaloo of the calypso, name dropping the archetypal village like the victimised Laventille, lamenting the rising death toll among the youth, and ended with the expected flamboyant flourish. Amidst the applause he stalked out furtively, looking around the audience to see whether Walcott, Strand or Brodsky were in the house. He thought he heard a loud steups somewhere from the dark.

Even as he stepped off the fabled Urn into the realm of modernity and contemporaneity, the music changed, the tempo quickened. He heard the music and it wasn't sweet. The pipes and timbrels became wilder and reached the wildest bacchanalian depths. Those unheard melodies became audible and not wild but sweet. They play to the inner ear, wittingly, as youth and old people, now living much longer, celebrate their sensuality almost to eternity. The goal is won over and over, repeatedly, everywhere, in sylvan locations, or in urban trappings: in parks, on beaches, against samaan trees, on river banks, on river stones, in motels, in hotels, in and out of marriage beds. Ecstasy and bliss become commonplace. Everyone is addicted. Bill is addicted. More bliss, more ecstasy is sought. The Grecian vessel is broken. The mystery and the marble have disappeared. In the age of transition and pastiche the verities have disappeared; though some are now said to be rallying around an old red house.

Anansi slinked on the ceiling like a ninja. He quietly settled in to capture a bellyful. Concentrating on his meal, he didn't notice the pole preparing to spear him. He heard the halal prayer. He sensed the kosher incantations, the Baraka Bashad blessings, as the giant prepared to send him to his next incarnation. Can't travel on hungry belly, he thought, dropping suddenly the precipitous distance, hitting the tiled floor, running on kilkitay legs, scurrying to the darkness, desperate to escape. Scurrying, hurrying into the darkened areas, too fast for the age-encumbered warrior, to escape in a crevice, terrified but alive; safe till another attempt at feeding.

Who knows another's realities? We live in so many parallel and private universes. Sometimes we briefly glimpse the other's worlds. Other worlds. Parents never know what the real world of the child is. Children manoeuvre around the adult's universe because they need succour from adults. Primal needs satisfied, they revert to their own activities, lives. Confusions, passions, truths are entirely different. Totally real. Much to the consternation of those who want every reality to be like theirs. Is the wife's reality the husband's? Are lovers' realities cloned? Siblings'? Twins'? Hindus', Muslims', Christians', Eckists'?

They spent the entire day knocking about. Sipped and chatted and walked and munched, catching up on the recent past and their family, till the rush hour was almost on them and they drove out of the city to a nearby town where she splurged on him at two sales outlets – a kind of pre-birthday gift. On the way home they stopped at the supermarket, where she bought him fruits and goodies. But most of all they talked and talked and talked and laughed and laughed and laughed. And riding home in her BMW convertible, going up hill and down dale on the highway, he felt as if it might have been the most delightful day of his life. A zen-like day where everything seems right – a frightening day too (for when you reach the mountain top the only other way is down). But it was a priceless father-daughter day – much as the special holiday they had when she was twelve.

Sugar down there. Brown sugar. Take a break. Take a bligh. Take a bligh in the sky. Look at all the TV ads. Radio ads. Newspaper ads. Magazine ads. Internet ads. All proclaiming the need for products to stop leakage. Smells. Itches. Germs. Diseases. Down there. Visit the sugar factory in Central. There, brown sugar is piled high on the bare floor for packaging. Brown sugar is good for you. Think diabetes and hypertension. Refined sugar is not good for you. But the packaging is great. It is as attractive as deodorant. Down there workmen just flick the sweat from their brows as they pile and package the stuff. Sometimes they hawk and spit. Girl, sugar down there. Think again.

The chela was helping out at a hospital. Elcock was dispensing and the chela was handing out the prescriptions. Elcock began to dance in a frenetic fashion while mixing his medicines. The crowd of patients got excited. In the crush of poor patients one woman's parcel was damaged. Outside a large crowd of stick-fighting women was demonstrating. Their drumming and chants further excited the patients. The women in the chela's line became sexually playful. One, who used to be a teacher but is now a librarian, wanted to play with the chela's rear. He hugged her to stop her. She suddenly grew ten feet tall and just as suddenly disappeared. The crowd of stick-fighting women and the patients disappeared. Elcock danced on.

When the chela returned to his table, a sumptuous repast was laid out. The donor was anonymous. Hooks were placed on the nearby wall and doors so that he could hang his things neatly. There was exercise equipment available. He had to train two young chelas. After the exercise he sat down to savour the delights. He shared them with people around. Some young men wanted sandwiches and roti instead of the exotic fare offered. The dishes were rich and were the kind of food the chela didn't consume except on rare occasions. He wanted to know what was the reason, what was the celebration. But he was thankful for the beneficence of Spirit.

Develop a culture of respecting psychic space. Respect the other's psychic space. One cannot be an individual and belong to another in that possessive sense. One cannot dispose of the other by violence if one wishes. People have to be taught to be secure in their selves. You are soul. He is soul. She is soul. We are soul. They are soul. Respect him. Respect her. Respect us. Respect them. Respect yourself. Love him. Love her. Love them. Love our selves. Love yourself. Love self.

The chela was searching for the temple near the Himalayas. In the foothills before the ascent he found a place to rest. While he was settling down a certain family decided to detain him. Women, sturdily built and fair, set two cobras to guard him. The smaller cobra made nibbling motions, but the larger one stood guard sternly, like the one that guarded the Buddha. The chela put his attention on the Soul Plane and held his ground. To the cobras he turned invisible. Confused, they grew bored and eventually fell asleep. Then he proceeded on his journey to the temple.

Beauty erupts before croptime starts and ratoons announce their time of fullness. Conical tassels dazzle the Xmas canescape. They shimmer like New Year's fireworks on January mornings that go out desultorily after their short-lived but glorious expressions of delight. Then, bitter toil begins; beauty bows to the slash of striking arms that lay her low in the cause of survival. Carts and trailers trundle, factory wheels grumble; heat converts reality to wealth. Soot spreads and covers beauty's place with a patina of Hades. From the nearby cremation site smoke darkens the sky.

There was a girl with a heart of gold. Her domed forehead shadowed soulful eyes. Her smile was sweet and tender. She had the spirit of an artist. She played games with him. Electronic table tennis on the drawing room tv set. Then she migrated and sent him a photograph inscribed, "Love always". It touched his heart. Then she disappeared for decades.

By the magic of the internet they rediscovered each other. Email bridged the gap of the years. The girl had blossomed into the golden girl of her potential. A beautiful artist woman in her prime, seasoned with the spice of experience. She shone in his heart. Resonated in his mind. She represented a dream long deferred. The one that dwells in the heart and mind. That reverberates in the senses. The soul. That girl. This woman. This soul. This golden love.

Day was disorienting for no special reason. It's kind of chilly, Trini style, early. The country is going crazy. All over, vibrations that he's alienated from crescendo and throb, making him melancholy. For him, for so many years it is a season of depression amidst the bacchanalian gaiety. His drummer is different, though he cannot fathom why. Only excesses of drink, romance, wild sex and constant frenzy would keep him apparently sane at this period. The last time that happened, decades ago, he couldn't account for many hours and all his actions. After that he dropped out and never drank again. Perhaps he's disoriented because a man on his street, pleasant Mr. Rollocks, to whom he had spoken the previous Wednesday, dropped dead suddenly; but mainly because it's carnival. As a Trini he should be happy, but he never is. "I grow old … I grow old … I shall wear the bottoms of my trousers rolled," as T.S. Eliot wrote, he ruminated.

As he stepped out to go to the newsstand, the platinum whiteness of the sun bathed the valley with its blessings. His neighbour's four red roses swayed resplendently in the air like beautiful dawn kisses. Mist on the hillsides was dissipating like a sweet lover's breath at the moment of parting. Day suddenly seemed so blessed and glorious that one could almost forget the security threat in a confrontation between Government and some would-be insurrectionists, who had threatened our civility and safety once before. It was a moment juxtaposed between sacred and profane. As he balanced on the cusp of an inexplicable emotion, he thought of his dear friend. When he returned, his spouse was watering her beloved flowers to save them from the scorching attentions of the Antillean eye in the sky.

Swami is serious about his dharma. Though in the last cycle of life, he clings mentally to those habits he should have moved beyond. He is vocal about the whole pantheon of gods, devtas, bhuts and prets, who need his input to protect their magnificence. Helpless gods they are in his eyes – he must destroy their enemies. So devotees rush out of houses of worship and even into houses of worship and destroy all in their way. They leave death and tragedy, pain and lamentation in their wake. Everywhere in churches, mosques, temples, in congregations mixed and single-sexed, with heads covered or uncovered, prostrate or kneeling, they wait for the services to end in order to storm out to their devotion of destruction. On a small scale it happened in this tiny country on July 27, 1990. Chanting the centuries old mantra to God, his greatness rending the air and detonating historical buildings, they spilled blood blood blood. In another huge country some helpless god commanded his devotees to immolate a trainload of pilgrims returning from service and satsang. At the site of the holy of holy they hear commands to reclaim a ruin or to ruin a reparation. Rubble is turned to rubble as they quarry martyrdom, sainthood or salvation.

When the historical buildings have been rebuilt, the trains have been scrapped and replaced, the rites and rituals performed, the swamis and their followers – their god having been served, praised, extolled and satisfied – harken for another cry from god for expiation.

## About the Author

Anson Gonzalez began his career as a poet in 1984. Since then his poems have been published in numerous journals, newsletters, newspapers, and anthologies. In the early '70s he began his life's work of promoting poetry and the literary culture of the Caribbean, and Trinidad and Tobago in particular. In 1973 he founded, edited, and published *The New Voices*, a bi-annual literary journal which has published poems, plays, short stories, and non-fiction by more than 300 Caribbean writers. *The New Voices* was published continuously for 21 years and was available upon request via electronic mail. One of the major accomplishments of *The New Voices* was the *Bibliography of Creative Writing in Trinidad & Tobago (1962-)*. In 1974 Anson Gonzalez established a publishing imprint called New Voices which published his own poetry collections and many other books by Caribbean writers. *The New Voices Newsletter* was founded in 1981 and served the Caribbean writing community for 12 years by providing information about writers, literary competitions, grants, and workshops.

One of the founders and former presidents of the Writers' Union of Trinidad and Tobago, Anson Gonzalez established the celebration of Poetry Day (October 15) in Trinidad and Tobago in 1979. The occasion is now observed annually in eight other Caribbean countries. In his continuing efforts to promote creative writing, he conducted two radio programmes, *Self-discovery through Literature* and *Trinidad and Tobago Literature: ON AIR*, designed to encourage the public to read the works of their country's authors. He has also conducted creative writing classes throughout the Caribbean, organized numerous literary competitions and poetry readings, obtained and awarded prizes to writers, and provided scholarships to writers' workshops. He has also judged many poetry writing and recitation competitions. He has been awarded the Writers' Union Writer of the Year Award (1988), and honoured for his services to the Caribbean literary community by the University of Miami.